The Countries

Canada

Christine Fournier
ABDO Publishing Company

visit us at
www.abdopub.com

Published by ABDO Publishing Company, 4940 Viking Drive, Edina, Minnesota 55435.
Copyright © 2002 by Abdo Consulting Group, Inc. International copyrights reserved in
all countries. No part of this book may be reproduced in any form without written
permission from the publisher.

Printed in the United States.

Photo Credits: Corbis
Art Direction & Maps: Neil Klinepier

Library of Congress Cataloging-in-Publication Data

Fournier, Christine, 1977-
   Canada / Christine Fournier.
      p. cm. -- (The countries)
   Includes index.
Summary: Provides an overview of the history, geography, people, economy,
government, and other aspects of life in Canada.
   ISBN 1-57765-751-9
      1. Canada--Juvenile literature. [1. Canada.] I. Title. II. Series.

   F1008.2 .F68 2002
   971--dc21

                                                         2001045896

Contents

Bonjour! 4

Fast Facts 6

Timeline 7

Canadian History 8

A Mighty Land 14

Plants & Wildlife 18

Canadians 20

The Economy 24

Cities 26

Across Canada 28

The Government 30

Festive Canadians 32

Sports & Arts 34

Glossary 38

Web Sites 39

Index 40

Bonjour!

Hello from Canada! Canada is the second-largest nation on Earth in area. Only Russia is bigger. Canada's land includes mountains, **glaciers**, hot springs, rivers, and **tundra**. Even during long winters, Canadians find ways to enjoy the outdoors.

The word Canada came from the Huron-Iroquois word *kanata*, meaning village or settlement. Explorers named Canada after the area around the settlement that is now Quebec city.

Canada's government is a **constitutional monarchy**. It is represented by the King or Queen of England. But a **prime minister** governs Canada.

Canada's first settlers were Native Americans. They began trading furs with Europeans. Since then, Canada has grown into an industrial nation. Its land is rich with minerals, oil, gas, and lumber. Canadians manufacture automobiles and high technology products.

Bonjour from Canada!

Canada is a growing country. With so much space,
and so many resources, its future looks promising.

Fast Facts

OTTAWA

OFFICIAL NAME: Canada
CAPITAL: Ottawa

LAND
- Mountain Ranges: Cordilleran, Appalacian, Innuitian
- Highest Peak: Mount Logan 19,524 feet (5,951 m)
- Major Rivers: Mackenzie, St. Lawrence
- Largest Lakes: Great Bear, Great Slave, Lake Winnipeg

PEOPLE
- Population: 31,698,000 (2002 est.)
- Major Cities: Toronto, Montreal, Vancouver, Edmonton
- Official Languages: English and French
- Religion: Christianity (Roman Catholicism and Protestantism)

GOVERNMENT
- Form: Constitutional monarchy
- Head of State: King or Queen of England
- Head of Government: Prime minister
- Legislature: House of Commons, Senate
- Flag: A red maple leaf on a white square, flanked by red bars.
- Other Symbols: A coat of arms with three maple leaves at the bottom. A unicorn and a lion stand on either side of the shield, with a smaller lion on top.
- Nationhood: 1931

ECONOMY
- Agricultural Products: Wheat, lumber
- Mining Products: Nickel, zinc, copper, iron ore, gold, lead, natural gas, petroleum
- Manufactured Products: Automobiles, machinery and equipment, high technology products
- Money: Canadian dollar (100 cents equals one dollar)

Canada's flag

Canada's units of currency are the dollar and the cent. The money is printed in English and French.

Timeline

1497	John Cabot finds rich fishing waters off Canada's southeast coast
1600s	About 200,000 Native Americans live in Canada
1608	Samuel de Champlain begins a colony near Quebec
1689-1763	French and English colonists fight four wars
1774	Quebec Act
1783	English loyalists move to Canada from colonies
1812-1815	The War of 1812
1867	British North American Act is signed; Dominion of Canada is formed; John A. Macdonald becomes first prime minister
1914-1918	World War I
1931	Statute of Westminster grants Canada independence
1939-1945	World War II
1964	Canada's new flag is approved
1967	100th anniversary of the Confederation; Expo '67
1969	Official Languages Act passes
1982	England and Canada sign Constitution Act
1992	North American Free Trade Agreement (NAFTA)
1999	Nunavut becomes a territory

Canadian History

Samuel de Champlain

In 1497, Italian explorer John Cabot found rich fishing waters off Canada's southeast coast. His discovery led to European exploration of Canada.

Canada's original settlers were Native Americans. In the 1600s, there were about 200,000 Native Americans living in Canada. The tribes included the Cree, Ojibwa, Blackfoot, Beaver, and Inuit.

The French were the first Europeans to settle Canada. Samuel de Champlain began a colony at present-day Quebec in 1608. The French called their North American land New France. They also called it Canada from the Huron-Iroquois word *kanata*, meaning village or settlement. The French began to trade with the Native Americans for furs.

In the late 1600s, England claimed land around the Hudson Bay. The English began to compete with the French in the fur trade.

The French and English colonists fought each other in four wars between 1689 and 1763. The first three wars were King William's War (1689-1697), Queen Anne's War (1702-1713), and King George's War (1744-1748). The fourth war began in the Ohio River Valley in 1754 and spread to Europe in 1756. It lasted until 1763, and is known as the Seven Years' War in Europe and Canada. In the United States, it is known as the French and Indian War.

These wars led to the United Kingdom's conquest of Canada. Through two treaties, the French lost all of their land east of the Mississippi to the English.

But the people of Quebec did not want to lose their French language and **culture**. So the English created the Quebec Act of 1774. It allowed the French Canadians to keep many French laws and customs. It also allowed Quebec to expand its boundaries.

In 1783, England lost its American colonies. But it kept its northern land. Many colonists who wanted to stay loyal to England moved to Canada.

The War of 1812 developed out of fighting in Europe between the United Kingdom and France. During this conflict, the British stopped U.S. ships bound for French ports. They seized British-born sailors. The United States declared war on Britain on June 18, 1812.

U.S. troops tried to capture Upper and Lower Canada during the war. But British and Canadian troops resisted the attacks. The war ended in 1815.

Canada's population rose sharply during the early 1800s as thousands of **immigrants** came from the United Kingdom. Canadians needed a strong central government to effectively rule their growing **confederation** of colonies.

The British North America Act, Canada's **constitution**, took effect on July 1, 1867. The **Dominion** of Canada was formed. It used the British

parliamentary form of government. John A. Macdonald was the first **prime minister**. But Canada still did not have complete independence from Britain.

John A. Macdonald

The **Dominion** of Canada developed rapidly during the late 1800s and early 1900s. Huge wheat crops, rich mines, and new industries brought **economic** growth. Canada became more involved in international affairs.

Canada entered World War I (1914-1918) to help Great Britain and its **allies**. For its participation in the war, Canada earned more power to form its own foreign **policies**.

In the late 1920s, Prime Minister W. L. Mackenzie King began pushing for independence. In 1931, the Dominion won complete independence from Great Britain when the British Parliament passed the **Statute** of Westminster.

During the 1930s, Canada suffered through the **Great Depression**. It ended when production rose during World War II (1939-1945). More than a million Canadian men and women served in the armed forces. Canadian troops fought bravely against the **Axis Powers** and helped the **Allies** win the war. Canada emerged as a major **economic** and political power in the late 1940s and through the 1950s.

The 1960s was an important decade for Canada. In 1964, the Canadian **Parliament** approved a new national flag design that featured a red maple leaf. On February 15, 1965, Canada's new flag flew for the first time.

Canada celebrated the 100th anniversary of the **Dominion** in 1967. The highlight was Expo '67, a world's fair held in Montreal that year.

In Quebec, many French Canadians wanted to make their **province** a separate nation. They did not gain independence. But Canada's government passed the Official Languages Act in 1969. It made French and English Canada's official languages.

In 1968, Pierre Elliott Trudeau became Canada's third French Canadian **prime minister**. Trudeau served almost continuously until 1984.

Brian Mulroney won the general election in September 1984. In 1988, Prime Minister Mulroney and U.S. President Ronald Reagan signed a free-trade agreement that ended all **tariffs** by 1999. In 1992, Canada signed the North American Free Trade Agreement (NAFTA) with the United States and Mexico. In late 1995 and early 1996, **Parliament** passed resolutions, or decisions, that promoted national unity.

Pierre Elliott Trudeau

A new territory called Nunavut came into being on April 1, 1999. The new territory provides more self-government for the Inuit.

A Mighty Land

Canada is the second-largest country in the world in area. Canada includes all of North America's land north of the United States, except Alaska. Canada's land has six different regions: the Canadian Shield, the interior plains, the lowlands, the Appalachian Mountains, the Western **Cordillera** (kor-dih-LAIR-uh), and the Arctic **Archipelago**.

The Canadian Shield is the largest of the regions. It covers half the nation's total area. Thousands of years ago, **glaciers** covered this area. The land is mostly flat and rocky, with many lakes.

The interior plains surround the Canadian Shield. They extend from the Arctic Ocean to the United States. The land

The Canadian Shield along the Slave River

DETAIL AREA

North America · Europe · Asia · Africa · South America · Australia · Antarctica

Alaska

CANADA

UNITED STATES

ARCTIC OCEAN

MOUNT LOGAN

Great Bear Lake

Great Slave Lake

PACIFIC OCEAN

WESTERN CORDILLERA

INTERIOR PLAINS

CANADIAN SHIELD

ARCTIC ARCHIPELAGO

Hudson Bay

Lake Winnipeg

APPALACHIAN MOUNTAINS

ATLANTIC OCEAN

LOWLANDS

The Great Lakes

St. Lawrence River

OTTAWA

ATLANTIC OCEAN

North · West · East · South

is flat, with several large lakes. Lake Winnipeg, one of Canada's largest lakes, is located there. The southern plains are the most fertile lands in Canada.

The lowlands surround the St. Lawrence River and stretch toward the Atlantic Ocean. Here, **glaciers** created rolling hills and lakes, including the Great Lakes. In some areas, the lowlands are good for farming.

The Appalachian Mountains extend north from eastern Quebec. The Western **Cordillera** are higher than the Appalachians. They are on Canada's Pacific coast. The Western Cordillera are made of numerous mountain groups, including the Canadian Rockies and the Columbia Mountains. Both mountain chains have **glaciers**, **fjords**, steep cliffs, and spectacular views. Mount Logan, Canada's highest mountain at 19,524 feet (5,951 m), is there.

Canada's Arctic **Archipelago** is made up of thousands of islands. They are north of Canada's mainland. Most of these are permanently covered with snow and ice.

Canada's climate ranges from long, cold winters to hot summers. The land near water has warmer winters and cooler summers. The interior land has cold winters and hot summers.

The Canadian Rockies

AVERAGE YEARLY RAINFALL

Rainfall

Inches		*Centimeters*
Under 8		*Under 20*
8 - 20		*20 - 50*
20 - 40		*50 - 100*
40 - 60		*100 - 150*
60 - 80		*150 - 200*
Over 80		*Over 200*

AVERAGE TEMPERATURE

Temperature

Fahrenheit		*Celsius*
Over 60°		*Over 15°*
50° - 60°		*10° - 15°*
40° - 50°		*4° - 10°*
10° - 40°		*-12° - 4°*
0° - 10°		*-18° - -12°*
-10° - 0°		*-23° - -18°*
-20° - -10°		*-29° - -23°*
Below -20°		*Below -29°*

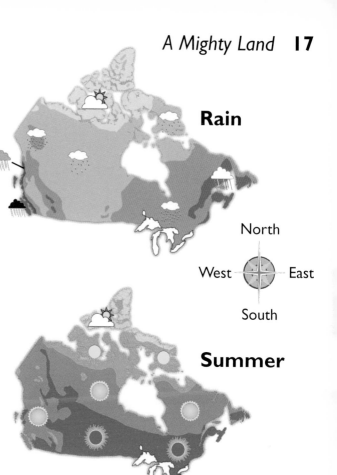

Rain

North

West — East

South

Summer

Winter

Plants & Wildlife

Canada's varied landscapes contain many types of plants and animals. Much of Canada is covered by **coniferous** forests. These forests contain spruce, white birch, balsam, fir, and tamarack trees.

Animals such as moose, bears, lynx, wolves, deer, and squirrels live in the northern forests. Birds such as Canada jays, gray jays, ravens, crows, and wild turkeys also live there.

Canada's Pacific Coast has forests with Douglas fir, western hemlock, and western red cedar trees. These forests are home to mountain sheep and goats, elk, and mule deer.

At the tops of Canada's mountains and in the arctic regions are the **tundra**. These areas have thin soil and few plants. Only **lichens**, mosses, and small shrubs can grow there.

Moss and lichen grow on the Canadian tundra.

Seals, polar bears, caribou, and musk oxen are some of the larger animals that live on the **tundra**. Smaller animals include lemmings, Arctic wolves, and white foxes. Birds such as Canada geese and snow geese travel to these cold areas to nest.

In the southern plains region, short grasses, sagebrush, and cacti are the main plants. In the northern plains, prairies cover the land. The land here is very fertile. Farmers can grow huge crops of wheat.

Animals such as ground squirrels and pocket gophers live on the plains. Badgers, hawks, and owls also live there. A few hundred years ago, bison roamed the prairie land. But today, hunters have driven the bison to near extinction. The large animals found on the prairie today include mule deer and pronghorn antelope.

A caribou on the tundra

Canadians

Canadians like to say that they are multicultural. They are proud of the many **cultures** that exist side by side in their country.

The largest **ethnic** population in Canada is European. Since Canada was a British colony for many years, British people outnumber any other group. The next largest group is the French. There are large numbers of Ukrainians and Italians, as well.

When the French settled, many of them had children with Native Americans. These people are called Métis. Many Native Americans and Métis live in Canada. There are more than 2,250 **reserves** in Canada. Each reserve governs itself. More than half of the Native Americans live on reserves.

Since 1960, Canada has allowed more people to

Métis drummers perform outside the Supreme Court Building in Ottawa.

immigrate. Now, Asian, Latin American, African, and Caribbean peoples are moving to Canada. The largest group of immigrants in Canada today is from Asia.

Canada is a **bilingual** country. Most French-speaking Canadians live in Quebec. Outside of Quebec, most Canadians speak English.

Almost half of all Canadians are Catholic. Other religions represented in Canada include Anglican and Lutheran. Almost all Canadians follow a religion.

Most Canadians live in or around cities. Many families live in houses. Single people often live in apartments. Some of Canada's rural people live and work on farms. Others work in fishing, mining, and lumbering industries. Many Inuit and Native Americans still fish, hunt, and trap. But traditional ways of life in the Arctic are ending.

A man pulls a child on a sled near the Chateau Frontenac in Quebec City.

Canadian **architecture** combines old and new. In Quebec, French styles of architecture are common. Toronto and Montreal have modern, sleek structures.

Canadian children must go to school from the ages of 6 or 7 until they are 15 or 16. Each **province** funds its own schools. In elementary school, students learn languages, math, social studies, art, and science. In secondary school, a student can prepare for a university, technical school, or the workplace.

The federal government helps students pay for general and **vocational** colleges. Less than half of Canadians go to some kind of school after high school.

Canadians eat foods similar to those eaten in the United States. They eat more beef than any other

Students at Vancouver's Strathcona School read a book together. They are learning English as a second language.

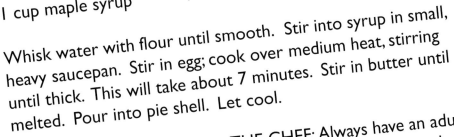

Maple Syrup Pie

1/2 cup cold water
1/4 cup flour
1 cup maple syrup

1 egg, lightly beaten
2 tablespoons butter
1 8-inch (20-cm) pie shell, baked

Whisk water with flour until smooth. Stir into syrup in small, heavy saucepan. Stir in egg; cook over medium heat, stirring until thick. This will take about 7 minutes. Stir in butter until melted. Pour into pie shell. Let cool.

AN IMPORTANT NOTE TO THE CHEF: Always have an adult help with the preparation and cooking of food. Never use kitchen utensils or appliances without adult permission and supervision.

meat. Bread and potatoes are common at dinner. Recently, Canadians have been adding native items such as elk, buffalo, chokecherries, and saskatoons to their diets. Also, many **immigrants** have brought Asian, German, and French **ethnic** foods to Canada.

The Economy

For many years, natural resources and agriculture supported Canada's **economy**. Canada's land is rich with lumber and wheat. And Canada's seas and lakes are stocked with fish. Canada also has oil, and minerals such as nickel, zinc, copper, and gold.

But today, Canada is an industrial society. Manufacturing, mining, and service industries now support its economy. Canada produces **petroleum**, manufactures transportation equipment, and processes paper, iron, and meat.

Canada trades many products with the United States and Mexico. In 1992, Canada joined them in signing the North American Free Trade Agreement (NAFTA). NAFTA allows Canada, Mexico, and the U.S. to trade without **tariffs**.

Canada also has a large tourism industry. People come from all around the world to see Canada's lakes, mountains, and **tundra**.

Canada's large size and small population make communication important. The government runs many communications companies. Most communication must be in English and French. The telephone, newspapers, radio, and the Internet all make communicating easy in Canada.

Canada's many lakes and rivers supply much of its energy. More than half of its electrical power comes from **hydroelectricity**. It produces enough energy to export some to the United States. Some of Canada's energy comes from coal, oil, and gas. Canada also uses energy from **nuclear** power plants.

A Canadian oil refinery

Cities

Most Canadians live in or around a city. Canada's largest city is Toronto, with more than four million people. Toronto is also Canada's most diverse city.

Many **immigrants** come to Toronto. It has a lot of **ethnic** neighborhoods, restaurants, and small businesses. Toronto has many museums and theaters. It is also home to the CN Tower, one of the world's tallest free-standing structures. It is 1,815 feet (553 meters) tall.

Montreal, the second-largest city, is the **cultural** center of the **province** of Quebec. Jacques Cartier claimed Montreal for France in 1535. Historic buildings and modern structures stand side by side in Montreal. The city has beautiful old churches, such as the Chapelle Notre-Dame-de-Bonsecours.

Montreal is also the second-largest French-speaking city in the world. It sits on an island in the St. Lawrence

River. Its position on the river makes it an excellent port city.

Vancouver, Canada's third-largest city, is one of the most scenic cities in the world. The Pacific Ocean is to the west, and there are mountains nearby. The city has a 1,000-acre (400-ha) park called Stanley Park.

Vancouver has a strong **economy**. It is Canada's busiest port. It has more banks, loan companies, and other financial institutions than any other city in western Canada.

The Toronto skyline

Across Canada

For hundreds of years, Canadians used the rivers and oceans to transport people and products. Native Americans and fur traders used canoes. Fishermen used boats, and loggers floated timber down rivers. Canadians were great shipbuilders. During this time, most Canadians lived near the water.

Beginning in the late 1800s, Canadians built railroads for transportation. In 1885, the first **transcontinental** railroad was completed. Today, the railroad systems are the Canadian National Railways and the Canadian Pacific Railways. Many people travel across Canada on these railroads.

Canadians also travel by car and airplane. Most Canadians and visitors drive in cars and ride buses. The Trans-Canada Highway passes through each of the 10

provinces. Regular bus lines transport people through the larger cities.

The Canadian government owns an airline called Air Canada. It is Canada's largest airline. It provides **domestic** and international service. There are also many privately owned airlines. These airlines are important since many parts of Canada can only be reached by air.

The Trans-Canada Highway

The Government

Canada's **constitution** is the 1867 British North America Act. It established Canada as a **constitutional monarchy**. In 1982, Canada and England passed the Constitution Act. It gave Canada the freedom to make changes to its constitution without approval from British **Parliament**.

The King or Queen of England is Canada's official head of state. He or she appoints a governor general to represent him or her in Canada. The governor general appoints a **prime minister**. As Canada's leader, the prime minister directs the Parliament's governing party and develops Canada's **domestic** and foreign policies.

The Parliament is the national **legislature** of Canada. It is made up of the **House of Commons** and the Senate.

The people elect the 301 members of the House of Commons. Each **province** has a certain number of members based on its population. The House of Commons makes laws and assigns a **budget** for all government programs.

The **prime minister** chooses 105 senators from all across Canada. The Senate **vetoes** or amends laws that the House has created.

Canada has 10 **provinces**: Newfoundland, New Brunswick, Prince Edward Island, Nova Scotia, Quebec, Ontario, Alberta, Saskatchewan, Manitoba, and British Columbia. It also has three territories: the Yukon Territory, the Northwest Territories, and Nunavut.

Each province has a lieutenant governor, who is appointed by the governor general and the prime minister. Each lieutenant governor has a premier and a **cabinet**. Each province also elects an assembly.

The three territories are governed by a government leader, an **executive council**, and the **Legislative** Assembly. The people elect the government leader and the Assembly. The Assembly chooses the Council members. Each territory sends one representative to the **House of Commons** in Ottawa.

The Canadian Parliament Building in Ottawa

Festive Canadians

Canadians celebrate many of the same holidays celebrated in the United States. They include Labor Day, Thanksgiving, Christmas, and New Year's Day. Canadians usually cook a large meal with a turkey on Thanksgiving, Christmas, and New Year's. French Canadians often cook a meat pie called *tourtiere*.

Canadians celebrate several unique holidays, as well. Canada Day is on July 1. This day marks the start of their **constitution**. They also celebrate Victoria Day in May. It honors the English queen who played a great role in Canada's history.

Quebec celebrates many Catholic holidays, such as Epiphany, Ash Wednesday, and Ascension Day. June 24 is Saint-Jean-Baptiste Day. This important

Miss Quebec wears her crown and robe in Montreal's Canada Day parade.

day is celebrated in honor of Saint-Jean-Baptiste, the Patron Saint of French Canadians.

Canadians celebrate many festivals. The Antigonish Highland Games take place in Nova Scotia. People play Scottish folk music and participate in heavyweight events like the **caber** toss. Montreal holds *Juste Pour Rire*, or Just for Laughs. It is the largest comedy festival in the world. Each July, the Calgary Stampede takes place in Calgary, Alberta. It is one of the world's biggest rodeos.

Many minority groups celebrate their **culture's** holidays as well. Chinese Canadians celebrate their New Year in February. They dance with colorful paper and fabric dragons down the streets of Toronto, Vancouver, and Victoria. Russian Canadians celebrate Peter's Day. They hold choral festivals to remember the reasons they left Russia to settle in Canada. Aboriginal Day in June is a time for all Canadians to recognize the cultural diversity and contribution of the Inuit, Métis, and other Native Americans.

Sports & Arts

Canadians enjoy exploring their country's vast landscapes. There are 29 national parks, and hundreds of **provincial** parks. Winter or summer, Canada's people find ways to enjoy their beautiful land.

During the long winters, Canadians enjoy sports such as ice hockey, tobogganing, and **curling**. Ice hockey originated in Canada in the mid-1800s. Today, ice hockey is an important sport in the Winter Olympic Games.

Canadians also practice activities such as ice skating and skiing. British Columbia and Quebec are popular for downhill skiing. Ottawa's Rideau Canal is crowded with ice skaters every year.

Canada has produced some of the greatest teams and players in professional hockey history.

In the summer, Canadians enjoy track and field games, baseball, golf, and lacrosse. Native Americans created lacrosse. In the 1800s, lacrosse was Canada's national game. Canada also holds the Canada Open golf tournament every year, which draws thousands of spectators. Canadians also hike, canoe, mountain climb, and picnic in their many beautiful parks.

Canada is known for great actors and writers. Novelist Margaret Atwood comes from Canada. Poet Alice Munro is a Canadian, as well. And Robert Service wrote poems about the Canadian gold-rush that have become famous. Finally, Canadian L. M. Montgomery wrote the *Anne of Green Gables* book series.

Chateau Lake Louise stands at the edge of Lake Louise in Banff National Park. It was built in 1923 to encourage travelers to visit the Canadian Rockies.

Many famous actors began their careers in Canada's theaters. Donald Sutherland and Michael J. Fox are two of them. The character Rambo was created by a Canadian.

Other Canadian performing arts include the ballet, orchestra, and opera. Montreal, Vancouver, and Toronto all have well-known orchestras. Canada's popular musicians include Bryan Adams, Celine Dion, Gordon Lightfoot, Alanis Morrissette, and Shania Twain.

Canada also has three professional ballet companies. They are the Royal Winnipeg Ballet, the National Ballet of Canada, and *Les Grands Ballets Canadiens*.

Canada's early artists painted images of Native Americans and Canadian landscapes. Painting is Canada's main visual art. But Canada's pioneers created totem pole carvings. And the Inuit created stone carvings.

Canada is a country with talented people, rich natural resources, and a rapidly developing government. Inside its vast boundaries, it has much to offer the world.

The Canadian Museum of Civilization near Ottawa is one of Canada's major museums. Its exhibits trace Canada's history and illustrate Inuit and other Native American cultures.

Glossary

allies - countries that agree to help each other in times of need. During World War II, Great Britain, France, the United States, and the Soviet Union were called the Allies.

Archipelago - a large group of islands.

architecture - the art of planning and designing buildings.

Axis Powers - During World War II, Germany, Italy, and Japan were called the Axis Powers.

bilingual - using or able to use two languages.

budget - the amount of money that is available for, required for, or assigned to a particular purpose.

caber - a long, heavy wooden pole tossed end over end as a demonstration of strength.

cabinet - a group of advisers chosen by the prime minister to lead government departments.

confederation - the body formed by persons, states, or nations united for support or common action.

coniferous - of or relating to a type of tree that bears needles or cones, and does not lose its leaves in the winter.

constitution - the laws that govern a country.

constitutional monarchy - a form of government ruled by a king or queen who must follow the laws of a constitution.

cordillera - a system of mountain ranges often consisting of a number of parallel chains.

culture - the customs, arts, and tools of a nation or people at a certain time.

curling - a Scottish game in which two four-person teams slide heavy stones into a circle at either end of a length of ice.

domestic - of, relating to, or originating within a country.

Dominion - a self-governing nation of the Commonwealth of Nations other than the United Kingdom that acknowledges the British monarch as chief of state.

economy - the way a state or nation uses its money, goods, and natural resources.

ethnic - of or having to do with a group of people who have the same race, nationality, or culture.

executive council - a council that advises or shares in the functions of a political executive.

fjords - a long, narrow, deep inlet of the sea between two steep slopes.

glacier - a large body of ice moving slowly down a slope or valley or spreading outward on a land surface.

Great Depression - a period of worldwide economic trouble (1929-1942) when there was little buying or selling and many people were out of work.

House of Commons - the lower house of the British and Canadian parliaments.

hydroelectric - the kind of electricity produced by water-powered generators.

immigrate - to come to a country to live.

legislature - the government branch that makes laws.

lichen - a moss-like plant.

nuclear - of or relating to atomic energy.

parliament - the highest lawmaking body of some governments.
petroleum - a thick, yellowish-black oil. It is the source of gasoline.
policy - a definite course or method of action used to make present and future decisions.
prime minister - the highest-ranked member of some governments.
province - one of the main divisions of a country.
reserve - a piece of land set aside by the government for Native Americans.
statute - a law made by the legislative branch of a government.
tariff - the taxes a government puts on imported or exported goods.
transcontinental - crossing a continent.
tundra - a vast, treeless plain.
veto - the right of one member of a decision-making group to stop an action by the group.
vocational - relating to or providing a special skill to be pursued in a trade, as a career.

English   French

LANGUAGE

Goodbye _____ Au revoir (ah-ray-VWAR)
Hello _____ Bonjour (bohn-JOOR)
No _____ Non (noh)
Please _____ S'il vous plait (seel-voo-PLAY)
Thank You _____ Merci (mehr-SEE)
Yes _____ Oui (WEE)
You're Welcome _____ De rien (duh-RAYUHN)

Web Sites

Canada's Digital Collections: http://collections.ic.gc.ca/
Check out Web sites created by students about everything Canadian, including government, history, first peoples, geography, and more. Also in French.

This site is subject to change. Go to your favorite search engine and type in Canada for more sites.

Index

A
animals 18, 19, 24
architecture 22, 26
Arctic Ocean 14
Atlantic Ocean 15

B
British 9, 10, 11, 20, 30
British North America Act 10, 30

C
Canadians 4, 13, 20, 21, 22, 23, 26, 28, 32, 33, 34, 35, 36
children 22
Chinese 33
cities 4, 21, 22, 26, 27, 33, 34, 36
climate 16
colonial wars 9, 10
colonies 8, 9, 10, 20
communication 25
constitution 10, 30, 32
culture 9, 20, 26, 32, 33, 34, 35, 36

D
Dominion of Canada 10, 11

E
economy 4, 11, 12, 24, 25, 27
education 22
energy 25
explorers 4, 8, 26

F
farms 11, 15, 19, 21, 24
festivals 33
food 22, 23, 32
French 8, 9, 10, 12, 13, 20, 22, 23, 25, 26, 32, 33

G
government 4, 10, 11, 12, 13, 20, 22, 25, 29, 30, 31, 36
Great Britain 9, 10, 11, 20, 30
Great Depression 12
Great Lakes 15

H
history 4, 8, 9, 10, 11, 12, 13
holidays 32, 33
houses 21

I
immigrants 10, 21, 23, 26
independence 11, 12
industry 4, 11, 21, 24, 25
Inuit 13, 21, 33, 36
Italians 20

K
King of England 4, 30
King, W. L. Mackenzie 11

L
Lake Winnipeg 15
lakes 14, 15, 24, 25
land 4, 14, 15, 16, 18, 19, 24, 34, 36
language 4, 8, 9, 12, 21, 25, 26

M
Macdonald, John A. 11
Métis 20, 33
Mexico 13, 24
mountains 4, 14, 16, 18, 24
Mulroney, Brian 13

N
national parks 34
Native Americans 4, 8, 20, 21, 28, 33, 35, 36

North American Free Trade Agreement (NAFTA) 13, 24

O
Official Languages Act 12

P
Pacific Ocean 27
plants 18, 19
provinces 8, 9, 12, 16, 21, 22, 26, 29, 30, 31, 33, 34, 36
provincial parks 34

Q
Quebec Act 9
Queen of England 4, 30

R
Reagan, Ronald 13
religion 21, 32, 33
rivers 15, 25, 27, 28
Russia 4, 14
Russians 33

S
sports 34, 35
Statute of Westminster 11

T
territories 13, 31
transportation 28, 29
Trudeau, Pierre Elliott 13

U
Ukrainians 20
United States 9, 10, 13, 14, 22, 24, 25, 32

W
World War I 11
World War II 12

Christmas in Germany

by Kristin Thoennes

Consultants:
Instructors of the Language Services Department
Germanic-American Institute

Hilltop Books

an imprint of Franklin Watts
A Division of Grolier Publishing
New York   London   Hong Kong   Sydney
Danbury, Connecticut

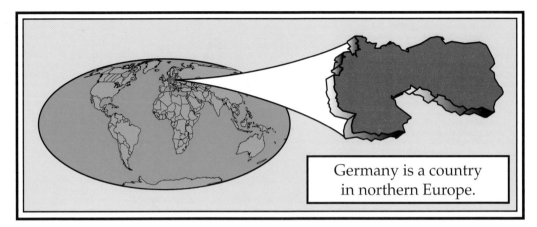

Germany is a country
in northern Europe.

Hilltop Books
http://publishing.grolier.com
Copyright © 1999 by Capstone Press. All rights reserved.
Published simultaneously in Canada. Printed in the United States of America.
No part of this book may be reproduced without written permission from the publisher.
The publisher takes no responsibility for the use of any of the materials or methods
described in this book, nor for the products thereof.

Library of Congress Cataloging-in-Publication Data
Thoennes, Kristin.
      Christmas in Germany/by Kristin Thoennes.
      p. cm.—(Christmas around the world)
      Includes bibliographical references and index.
      Summary: An overview of the symbols, celebrations, decorations, food, and songs that are part of Christmas in
Germany.
      ISBN 0-7368-0089-1
      1. Christmas—Germany—Juvenile literature. 2. Germany—Social life and customs—Juvenile literature.
[1. Christmas—Germany. 2. Germany—Social life and customs. 3. Holidays.] I. Title. II. Series.
GT4987.49.T56 1999
394.2663'0943—dc21
                                                                      98-16202
                                                                         CIP
                                                                          AC

Editorial Credits
Michelle L. Norstad, editor; James Franklin, cover designer and illustrator;
   Sheri Gosewisch, photo researcher

Photo Credits
Gerhard Gscheidle, 4, 12. Keystone, 10, 16, 18. Photo Researchers/David Kraus, cover;
Josef Ege, 20.
Trip Photo Library/F. Lulinksi, 8, 14, Unicorn Stock Photos/D & I MacDonald, 6.

Table of Contents

Christmas in Germany 5

The First Christmas. 7

Christmas Trees 9

Decorations 11

Christmas Celebrations. 13

Saint Nicholas 15

Christmas Presents 17

Holiday Foods 19

Christmas Songs 21

Hands on: Make Your Own Christmas Tree 22

Words to Know 23

Read More 24

Useful Addresses and Internet Sites 24

Index. 24

Christmas in Germany

Many people around the world celebrate Christmas. Celebrate means to do something enjoyable on a special occasion. People in different countries celebrate Christmas in different ways.

Germany is a country in northern Europe. People from Germany are Germans. They speak the German language. Their Christmas greeting is Fröhliche Weihnachten (FROH-lik-uh VEYE-nahkt-en). It means Merry Christmas.

Germans celebrate Christmas Day on December 25. But Germans begin celebrating the Christmas season four weeks before Christmas Day. The Christmas season in Germany ends on January 6. Germans call this day Epiphany or Three King's Day.

The weather in Germany at Christmas time is cold. The temperatures are near freezing on some days. Snow covers much of the country.

Germans begin celebrating the Christmas season four weeks before Christmas Day.

The First Christmas

Many people who celebrate Christmas are Christians. A Christian is a person who follows the teachings of Jesus Christ. Christians celebrate Jesus' birthday on Christmas Day.

Christians tell the story of the day Jesus was born. Mary was Jesus' mother. Joseph was her husband. Mary and Joseph traveled to the town of Bethlehem. They could not find a room at any of the inns. An inn is like a hotel. Mary and Joseph had to stay in a building for animals called a stable. Jesus was born in the stable.

Jesus' first bed was a manger. A manger is a food box for animals. Mary and Joseph put straw in the manger. The straw kept Jesus warm.

Three kings saw a bright star the night Jesus was born. The kings followed the star to the stable. They brought gifts for Jesus.

Jesus was born in a stable.

Christmas Trees

Christmas trees are symbols of Christmas in Germany. A symbol is an object that reminds people of something important. The German word for Christmas tree is Tannenbaum (TAH-nuhn-bawm). Germans were the first people to use Christmas trees.

Many stories tell about how evergreen trees became Christmas trees. Most evergreen trees are pine trees. One story says Germans believed both evergreen trees and lights kept away bad spirits. During the 12 days of Christmas, Germans put candles on the evergreens to keep away bad spirits.

Another story tells about a German minister named Martin Luther. A minister is a person who leads a church. Martin walked in a forest one starry Christmas Eve. He thought the evergreens and stars were beautiful. Martin cut down an evergreen tree and put candles on it. Martin thought the candlelight looked like stars.

Christmas trees are symbols of Christmas in Germany.

Decorations

Germans put many types of decorations on Christmas trees. They use thin pieces of shiny metal or paper called tinsel. They put candles, stars, or angels on Christmas trees. Germans also may use baked decorations called Lebkuchen (LAYB-kook-en).

Many Germans hang strings of lights outside. They hang lights on lampposts, houses, and store fronts.

Germans decorate with Advent wreaths. An Advent wreath is a circle of greenery with four candles. People light one candle the first week. They light two candles the second week and three the third week. People light all four candles the fourth week.

The Advent calendar is another popular German decoration. An Advent calendar has doors on it. Each door covers one day from December 1 to Christmas Day. Children open one door each day. Pictures, treats, or small gifts may lie behind the doors.

Germans decorate with Advent wreaths.

Christmas Celebrations

Many Germans celebrate Christmas at Christmas markets. People hear songs and music at these markets. Germans can watch puppet shows and plays. Shoppers can buy food, toys, and Christmas decorations.

Germans celebrate many holidays during the Christmas season. They celebrate Saint Nicholas Day on December 6. Saint Nicholas is the saint for children.

The Christmas tree is an important part of German celebrations. Parents spend Christmas Eve decorating the tree. Children wait in another room until they hear a bell. Then parents bring their children into the room. The children see their presents under the decorated tree.

Germans also celebrate the Second Day of Christmas. This holiday is on December 26. Many Germans spend this day with family and friends.

Germans celebrate New Year's Day on January 1. People welcome the new year with parties, fireworks, and music.

Many Germans celebrate Christmas at Christmas markets.

Saint Nicholas

Many German children believe in Saint Nicholas. Saint Nicholas wears a red robe and a pointed hat. He also has a white beard and carries a cane. Children leave their shoes out for Saint Nicholas on December 5. The next day, they find their shoes filled with toys and treats.

Some children also believe in the Weihnachtsmann (VEYE-nakts-mahn). Weihnachtsmann means Christmas man. He looks like Saint Nicholas. The Weihnachtsmann brings gifts on Christmas Eve.

Some children write letters to the Cristkind (KRISS-kind). The Cristkind is the baby Jesus. Children may write letters to ask for gifts. Some children put the letters on a windowsill. Sometimes children make their letters sparkle. They put glue on the letters. Then they sprinkle sugar on the glue.

The Weihnachtsmann brings gifts on Christmas Eve.

Christmas Presents

Germans give presents at Christmas time. Presents remind Germans of the three kings' gifts. The three kings brought presents to Jesus when he was born.

Family members give each other presents on Christmas Eve. Some families read about Jesus' birth before opening presents. Families do this to remember Jesus on his birthday.

Germans spend Christmas Day and December 26 with friends and family. Children receive presents from aunts, uncles, and grandparents. They also may receive presents from friends.

German children receive many kinds of presents. They may receive dolls, trains, or jewelry such as rings and necklaces. They also may receive clothes, books, or games.

German children receive many kinds of presents.

Holiday Foods

Families in Germany eat many different foods during the Christmas season. Some families eat roast goose or roast pork. Others may eat turkey or duck. Carp is another popular Christmas food. Carp is fish.

A popular treat in Germany is Lebkuchen. Lebkuchen is gingerbread. Some people use Lebkuchen as decorations. They make Lebkuchen cookies shaped like stars or bells. They hang the Lebkuchen cookies on Christmas trees.

Gingerbread houses are popular in Germany. Germans make them with Lebkuchen. They decorate the gingerbread houses with frosting and candy.

Another popular treat is marzipan (MAIR-zi-pan). Marzipan is a candy made of roasted almonds and sugar. Many Germans enjoy the taste of marzipan.

Gingerbread houses are very popular in Germany.

Christmas Songs

Germans wrote many Christmas songs. Several are popular all over the world. One song is "Oh Christmas Tree." Another song is "Silent Night, Holy Night." "Hark! The Herald Angels Sing" is also a Christmas song from Germany.

Christmas caroling is popular in Germany. Years ago, poor Germans caroled from house to house. They sang outside each house. People sometimes gave the singers small gifts. Many Germans still enjoy Christmas caroling today.

Many German town bands play songs during the Christmas season. The bands play music in town squares. They also play songs in churches.

Many Germans go to church services on Christmas Eve. They sing songs together at church services. They also listen to music.

Many Germans go to church services on Christmas Eve.

Hands on: Make Your Own Christmas Tree

The Christmas tree is an important symbol in Germany. You can grow a small Christmas tree.

What You Need

One large pinecone   Soil
One large bowl   Grass seed
Water   Scissors
One large jar

What You Do

1) Remove any stem from the pinecone. Do this so the cone will stand up.
2) Fill the bowl with warm water. Soak the pinecone in the water for 10 minutes.
3) Put one inch (2.5 centimeters) of water in the jar.
4) Remove the pinecone from the bowl and put it in the jar.
5) Sprinkle soil onto the pinecone.
6) Sprinkle grass seed onto the pinecone.
7) Put the jar in a sunny place.
8) Check the water level often. Add water if the level is below one inch (2.5 centimeters).
9) Check your pinecone every day. Watch the grass grow on your pinecone. The pinecone will look like a Christmas tree. Trim the grass with a scissors when it becomes long.

Words to Know

Advent wreath (AD-vent REETH)—a circle of greenery with four candles

celebrate (SEL-uh-brate)—to do something enjoyable on a special occasion

Christian (KRISS-chuhn)—a person who follows the teachings of Jeus Christ

evergreen (EV-ur-green)—a tree that stays green all year

Fröhliche Weihnachten (FROH-lik-uh VEYE-nahkt-en)—the German phrase for Merry Christmas

Lebkuchen (LAYB-kook-en)—gingerbread

manger (MAYN-jur)—a food box for animals

minister (MIN-uh-stur)—a person that leads a church

stable (STAY-buhl)—a building for animals

symbol (SIM-buhl)—an object that reminds people of something important

tinsel (TIN-suhl)—a thin piece of paper or metal that shines

Read More

Christmas in Today's Germany. Christmas around the World from World Book. Chicago: World Book, 1993.

Lankford, Mary. *Christmas around the World.* New York: Morrow Junior Books, 1995.

Naythons, Matthew. *Christmas around the World.* San Francisco: Collins Publishers, 1996.

Useful Addresses and Internet Sites

The German Embassy
4645 Reservoir Road
Washington, DC 20007

Germanic-American Institute
301 Summit Avenue
St. Paul, MN 55102

Christmas in Germany
http://www.germanembassyottawa.org/Christmas/index.html
Christmas in Germany
http://www.germany-info.org/gnew/christmas/christmas.htm
Santa's Favorites: Around the World
http://www.santas.net/germanchristmas.htm

Index

Advent calendar, 11
Advent wreath, 11
candles, 9, 11
Cristkind, 15
Christmas markets, 13
decorations, 11, 13, 19
Jesus, 7, 15, 17
Lebkuchen, 11, 19

manger, 7
marzipan, 19
Saint Nicholas, 13, 15
songs, 21
star, 7, 11, 19
three kings, 7, 17
tree, 9, 11, 13, 19
Weihnachtsmann, 15